hc

Comets, Asteroids and Meteors

Steve Parker

WAYLAND

First published in Great Britain in 2007
By Wayland, an imprint of Hachette Children's Books
Hachette Children's Books
338 Euston Road, London NW1 3BH

Editor: Nicola Edwards
Designer: Tim Mayer
Consultant: Ian Graham

British Library Cataloguing in Publication Data
Parker, Steve
   Comets, asteroids and meteors. - (Earth and space)
   1. Comets - Juvenile literature
   2. Asteroids - Juvenile literature
   3. Meteors - Juvenile literature
   I. Title
   523.5

ISBN-13: 9780750249232

Cover photograph: A meteor shower, taken over
many minutes. The photograph shows ordinary stars
moving as slightly curved streaks.

Photo credits: Michael Abbey/SPL: 35; Julian
Baum/New Scientist/SPL: 17; Bettmann/Corbis: 14;
Jonathan Blair/Corbis: 34; Chris Butler/SPL: 18; Peter
Casolino/Sygma/Corbis: 5; Dennis di Cicco/SPL: 12;
Dreamworks/Paramount/The Kobal Collection: 24;
ESA: 9; ESA/AOES Medialab: 8; Dr Fred Espenak/SPL:
front cover, 32; Mark Garlick/SPL: 26; A.
Gragera/Latin Stock/SPL: 43; Victor Habbick
Visions/SPL: 33; Hayabusa: 41; John Hopkins
University Applied Physics Lab/Southwest Research
Institute: 27; John Hopkins University Applied Physics
Lab/SPL: 23; JPL/Cal-Tech/NASA: 7; JPL/UMD/NASA:
40; © Keck Observatory: 21; Mehau Kulyk/SPL: 1,31;
Claus Lunau/Foci/Bonnier Publications/SPL: 11; Gianni
Dagli Orti/Corbis: 13; NASA: 15, 16, 29, 42;
NASA/ESA/STSCI/B.Zellner; GSU/SPL: 20; NASA/SPL:
10, 19, 22, 37; Pekka Parviainen/SPL: 28;
Picturepoint/Topfoto: 45; Roger Ressmeyer/Corbis: 4,
38; Reuters/Corbis: 30; D. Roddy, CUS Geological
Survey, Lunar & Planetary Institute: 36; Dennis
Scott/Corbis: 25; WIYN/NOAO/AURA/NSF/epa/Corbis:
6; Frank Zullo/SPL: 39.

Contents

Smaller Objects in Space

Most of the objects we see in the night sky are huge. Twinkling stars look tiny because they are so far away. But some are thousands of times bigger than our nearest star, the Sun. Much closer to home than the stars are smaller objects in space. They may be relatively tiny. But they provide fascinating information about the Sun, the Earth and the other planets, as well as how all these objects began – and how they might end.

The Solar System

The Sun is a star – a massive object in space that gives off energy, mainly light and heat. The Earth is a planet – a relatively large object that goes around, or orbits, a star. In Earth's case, the star is the Sun. A moon (such as Earth's Moon) is an object that orbits a planet. Our neighbouring planet Mars has two moons, while the huge planet Jupiter has more than 60. The Sun, all of its planets, and all of their moons, form most of the Solar System.

Types of smaller objects

Apart from the Sun, its planets and their moons, there are other kinds of objects in the Solar System. Three of these are comets, asteroids and meteoroids.

The Galileo *space probe took this close-up photograph of the asteroid Ida in 1993.*

Comets are small lumps of mixed dust, frozen 'ice' and other bits and pieces which may follow very long, lop-sided orbits around the Sun. They come near to the Sun, then head out into the depths of the Solar System or beyond, before heading back to the Sun again. Other comets pass by the Sun once, never to return.

Asteroids are rocky lumps, smaller than planets, which go around the Sun. Sometimes they are called 'minor planets' or 'planetoids'. Most asteroids orbit in the wide gap between the planets Mars and Jupiter.

Meteoroids burn up near Earth as 'shooting stars'.

Meteoroids are little pieces of rock and other substances which are smaller than asteroids. Most are tinier than grains of sand or bits of dust. Some meteoroids orbit the Sun, while others whizz through space on random paths through the Solar System.

In 2006 a world gathering of space experts decided that comets, asteroids, meteoroids and similar objects orbiting the Sun, that were not planets or moons, should all be known by the general name of Small Solar System Bodies, SSSBs or 'S3Bs'.

SPACE DATA

Here are some sizes of space objects to compare:

	Diameter (distance across)
Sun (a star)	1,392,000 km
Jupiter (the biggest planet)	142,900 km
Earth	12,756 km
Mercury (the smallest planet)	4,880 km
Moon (Earth's Moon)	3,480 km
Pallas (biggest asteroid)	540 km
Halley's Comet (its central core or nucleus)	15 km
Meteoroids	Vary greatly but usually metres to fractions of a millimetre

Comet Heads and Tails

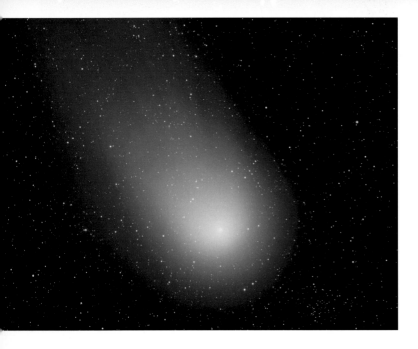

The name of this comet, C/2001 Q4 (NEAT), shows it was discovered in the year 2001 by the Near-Earth Asteroid Tracking organization, NEAT.

Space Facts

A comet's coma and tails can be truly vast.

● Most comas are around 100,000 kilometres across.

● Some comas are more than 1.5 million kilometres across, which is bigger than the Sun.

● Some tails are 150 million kilometres long – the same distance as from the Earth to the Sun.

● Two of the longest tails, at 570 million kilometres, belonged to the very bright Comet Hyakutake in 1996.

Comets are mysterious space objects that shine in the night sky, with a front end or head, and a long, streak-like, glowing tail. Some are unexpected and appear from nowhere. Others come back time and again after gaps of years. We can predict their appearance to within days or even hours.

What do comets look like?

A typical comet has a small, solid lump in its head, called its nucleus (see page 8). When we view a comet from Earth, the nucleus is far too small to make out. What we see are other parts of a comet. These are its coma and its tail. In fact there are usually two tails, one made from dust and one of gas.

The comet's coma

Earth has a layer of air around it, called the atmosphere. A comet has an atmosphere too, although this is much thinner and more wispy than around Earth, and it extends much farther out into space. A comet's atmosphere is called the coma and it surrounds the nucleus as a glow. It is made of dust and gases given off by the nucleus as this is heated by the Sun.

This drawing shows how the centre or nucleus of Comet Wild 2 might have looked, as the Stardust *space probe passed in January 2004.*

The Sun sends out powerful amounts of ray and wave energy, or radiation, including light rays and heat (infra-red) waves. The Sun also sends out streams of particles called the solar wind. Both the radiation and solar wind leave the Sun in all directions, streaming out into deep space.

Two tails

The radiation and particles from the Sun 'blow' the comet's thin, flimsy coma into one or more tails, spreading out from the head. The tails do not trail behind the comet as it zooms along. They always point away from the Sun.

One type of tail is the dust tail. This may be slightly curved, due to the comet's fast movement through space. The other type of tail is the gas tail. This is usually straight because the gas is lighter and blown more strongly by the Sun. The dust tail shines because its bits of dust reflect or bounce back sunlight. The gas tail glows because the gas particles in it themselves give out light.

How do we know?

Comet collection

The *Stardust* spacecraft was launched in 1999 to collect particles of the solar wind, which the Sun 'blows' out into space. But it also passed near to Comet Wild 2 in 2004 and collected particles of its coma. *Stardust* brought these samples in a container back to Earth in January 2006. The tiny bits of dust show that the comet is as old as the Solar System itself, 4.5 billion years. They contain substances such as iron, chemicals called sulphides, and shiny greenish-yellow crystals of a rock mineral, olivine.

Inside a Comet

Ideas about comets have changed greatly over the years. In particular, long-travelling spacecraft have made exciting discoveries during the past few years. These finds have helped to answer the mystery of what is inside a comet and show how it changes as it travels nearer to the Sun and then away again.

Changing ideas

In the middle of a comet's head is its nucleus – a small, very dark lump. Most comet nuclei are less than 50 kilometres across. An early scientific suggestion was that the nucleus of a comet was a 'gravel bank' of bits of stones like small pebbles, contained in a layer of ice. In 1950, US astronomer Fred Whipple suggested the famous 'dirty snowball' idea. This described the nucleus as small bits of dust and other rocky debris mixed into a huge lump of ice. The ice was not simply frozen water but other frozen substances too, like methane, carbon dioxide and ammonia (which are gases here on Earth).

Space Facts

Comet nuclei

● Comet nuclei vary greatly in size. Comet Hale-Bopp's nucleus is 40 km across, while Comet Hyakutake's nucleus is 2 km across.

● Most comet nuclei are between 1 and 50 km across.

A lander from the space probe Rosetta *should touch down on Comet Churyumov-Gerasimenko in the year 2014.*

In 2005 the spacecraft *Deep Impact* sent a small 'impactor' to smash into the surface of the nucleus of Comet Tempel 1. The results showed that the nucleus contained less ice than previously thought, and more dust and rocky particles. So the description of a comet nucleus has changed from a 'dirty snowball', with more ice than dust, to an 'icy dirtball', with more rocky debris and dust than ice.

Switched on

A comet does not always have its coma and tails. In deep space it is just the nucleus – a small, dark lump like a blob of road tarmac. It only starts to form its coma and tails when it comes near enough to the warmth of the Sun to heat up and 'switch on'. This usually happens when the nucleus enters an area of the Solar System which is closer to the Sun than Jupiter. Then the surface of the nucleus begins to warm up. Cracks appear and jets of gas blast out, carrying dust and chunks of rock. The comet grows its coma, looking like a fuzzy star. Then its tails form and grow longer as the comet nears the Sun.

The Giotto *probe was launched in July 1985 and passed within 600 kilometres of Halley's Comet in March 1986.*

After the comet curves around the Sun, it gradually becomes cooler as it travels away. Its tails shorten, its coma fades, and the surface of its nucleus, now too cold to spurt out dust and gas, becomes calm and still. Finally the comet 'switches off' as it heads away to the cold darkness of deep space.

How do we know?
Halley's Comet
During Halley's Comet's last visit in 1986, the *Giotto* spacecraft flew past and sent back close-up pictures of its almost black nucleus sending out jets of gas and spurts of dust. Other craft that have visited Halley's Comet include *Vegas 1* and *2*, and *Sakigake* and *Suisei*.

9

Comets' Journeys

Some comets are seen only once, and then disappear into deep space. Others return every so often, coming around on the same familiar pathway. Astronomers (experts on objects and events in space) can follow a comet's movements to find out where it has been as well as where it is heading and how long it will take to get there.

Regular and irregular visitors

Comets that appear only once and then travel away on a non-return path are known as single-pass, single-apparition or nonperiodic comets. They may simply zoom through space for ever, or perhaps smash into another space object such as a planet.

Comet Encke was discovered by Jean Louis Pons, but named after Johann Franz Encke, who worked out its orbit time.

Comets that return regularly to loop around or orbit the Sun are known as periodic comets. Most are in very long, elliptical (oval) paths or orbits, with the Sun within one end of the orbit, pulling the comet with its immense gravity. The final fates of comets vary. Some crash into planets, moons, asteroids or the Sun itself. Others break up into small fragments or gradually burn away after several passes around the Sun.

The long and the short

Short-period comets complete one orbit in less than 200 years. Long-period comets take more than 200 years for an orbit. This means that long-period comets discovered within the past 200 years have yet to return. But astronomers can work out their orbital time or period from the comet's speed and its curved pathway.

SPACE DATA

Comets vary in the time they take to complete one orbit:

Comet Encke	3 years 4 months (one of the shortest)
Comet Biela	6 years 7 months
Comet Tempel-Tuttle	33 years
Halley's Comet	76 years
Comet Hale-Bopp	2,380 years
Comet West	500,000 years

Where do comets orbit?

The planets of the Solar System orbit the Sun in the same plane or level, as though they are spread out on a circular table top. Comets are found not just in this plane. They orbit the Sun at many different angles – that is, above and below the 'table top'.

Most short-period comets probably orbit from near the Sun out to the Kuiper Belt. This is a zone of space objects beyond the planet Neptune (see page 26). The orbits of most long-period comets probably extend much farther, into the Oort Cloud. This is a vast ball-like 'shell' of objects at the edge of the Solar System, thousands of times more distant than the planets farthest from the Sun. The Oort Cloud may be the home of trillions of 'sleeping' comets. Every now and then, one is pulled inwards and begins its immense journey into the Solar System.

Comets may loop around the Sun, 'graze' past it, or head out into deep space (lower left).

Comets in History

Comets have fascinated people since ancient times. They appeared as if from nowhere, shining in the night sky and following strange paths, unlike the Moon and stars. No wonder they were linked with gods and spirits – usually as bringers of evil.

Space Facts

Comet Biela

- Comet Biela was one of the first comets to be shown as periodic – a regular visitor. It was first seen in 1772 and regularly every 6.6 years from then.

- During its 1846 passage it seemed to break into two. These pieces were seen separately in 1852 but never again.

Hairy stars

Aristotle of Ancient Greece helped to invent the word 'comet'. It comes from a Greek term komet meaning 'hair', and Aristotle referred to comets as 'stars with hair'. For centuries comets, like eclipses, were thought to be mysterious chariots of the gods, perhaps visiting Earth to take revenge, or maybe aliens from another world, or evil spirits. Some people offered gifts and carried out sacrifices of animals and people, to appease the comet-god so that it would go away – which it always did.

In the air or up in space?

Early astronomers thought that comets were, like clouds, within the Earth's layer of air, the atmosphere. But the studies of the Danish scientist Tycho Brahe in the 1500s and the English astronomer Edmund Halley in the late 1600s and early 1700s showed that they were far above Earth, in space like the Moon, Sun and stars. Halley was excited by the so-called Great Comet of 1680, one of the brightest ever. He had the new idea that each comet sighting, as recorded by astronomers for centuries, might not always be a 'new' comet. It could be an 'old' one coming back at regular intervals.

Comet Kohoutek, named after Czech astronomer Lubos Kohoutek, went past Earth in 1973 – and will come back in 75,000 years.

Halley's Comet

Edmund Halley worked out that sightings in 1531, 1607 and 1682 could all be the same comet. He predicted it would return in 1758 after another gap of 76 years. He was right and the comet was named after him. (He never saw it, since he died 16 years earlier.) Working backwards into history, astronomers found that Halley's Comet has been sighted for more than 2,200 years. It is shown in the background of the Bayeux Tapestry, which records William the Conqueror's invasion of England under King Harold, in 1066.

In 1066 Halley's Comet was called a 'comet-star' and believed to bring bad luck – which it did to King Harold.

How do we know?

Discovering comets

As we build improved telescopes and launch more technically advanced spacecraft, hundreds of new comets are now being discovered every year. The *SOHO* satellite (SOlar and Heliospheric Observatory) orbits the Sun about 1.5 million kilometres away from Earth. Its main task is to study the Sun but since its launch in 1995 it has discovered well over 1,000 comets.

Naming Comets

Edmund Halley (1656-1742) was British Astronomer Royal from 1720 until his death.

For many years after the naming of Halley's Comet, comets were named after people – usually their discoverers. But as more are identified, sometimes dozens in a week, this method has become very difficult. So a proper scientific naming system runs alongside the 'everyday' one.

An everlasting name

Centuries ago, comets were named after the year in which they appeared, and also some feature of their visit, such as the September Comet of 1882 or the Daylight Comet of January 1910 (so called because of its immense brightness). The tradition also grew of naming a comet after the person who first discovered it or observed its orbit, if this person was known. Halley's Comet was the first to have a widespread 'human name', from about 1759.

The tradition for naming a comet after the person who first spotted it means that comets are a great way for amateur astronomers to make an 'everlasting' name for themselves. It is very difficult even for professional astronomers to predict when and where a comet will appear. So hobbyist stargazers have a chance of spotting a comet before the professionals discover it.

Space Facts

Comet Tuttle-Giacobini-Kresak was discovered three times:

- By Horace Tuttle in 1858,
- By Michel Giacobini in 1907.
- By Lubor Kresak in 1951.
- This comet is one of the 'Jupiter family', meaning that its farthest point from the Sun is near the planet Jupiter.
- It flares up brightly now and again, the last major flare being in 1973.

Usually up to three names are allowed for this 'unofficial' system. If the same person or people discover several comets, then these are given numbers. The Shoemaker-Levy comets (see panel) were found by Carolyn Shoemaker and David Levy, using a wide-viewing telescope at the Palomar Observatory, California, USA. (Levy has a double honour – an asteroid is also named after him.)

Space Facts

Orbiting Jupiter

- In March 1993 Shoemaker and Levy discovered a new comet, provisionally named Shoemaker-Levy 9.

- This was the first comet discovered that was not orbiting the Sun. It was going around planet Jupiter.

- Also it was not a single lump or nucleus, but had broken into 20-plus pieces or fragments, the largest being about two kilometres across.

- During mid July 1994, the fragments plunged into Jupiter at speeds of up to 60 kilometres per second.

- The collisions caused massive storm-like disturbances which could still be seen on Jupiter months later.

Discovered by machine

Some comets are discovered by huge teams of astronomers with very specialist equipment. The equipment sometimes gets a mention in the naming. Comet IRAS-Araki-Alcock was found by the *IRAS* satellite and separately by Genichi Araki and George Alcock.

Alongside this 'unofficial' system, which is easy for most people to understand, astronomers also have an official number-and-letter system for naming comets. This shows the order of their discovery compared to other comets, and tracks the year of each visit. In this system Halley's Comet is known as 1P/Halley (P = Periodic) and the code for its last appearance in 1986 is 1P/1986III.

Dark patches near the bottom of Jupiter show where pieces of Comet Shoemaker-Levy 9 plunged into its swirling gases.

How Asteroids were Formed

Asteroids are rocky lumps less than 1,000 kilometres across that, like the planets, whirl around the Sun. They were formed at the same time as the rest of the Solar System. Most asteroids are found in a zone called the Asteroid Belt or Main Belt. This occupies the large gap between the last of the small inner planets, Mars, and the first of the giant outer planets, Jupiter.

Origin of asteroids

The whole Solar System probably formed about 4,600 million years ago. A vast cloud of gas and dust floating in space, called a nebula, gradually started to clump together into larger lumps. This clumping may have been caused by the explosion of a nearby star, known as a supernova. Attracted to each other by the force called gravity, the lumps formed a tighter ball shape which began to whirl around like a spinning top.

This telescope view shows the largest asteroid, Pallas, among groups of stars indicated by the M (Messier) and NGC (New General Catalogue) code numbers.

How do we know?
Filling the gap

In 1800 a group of astronomers called the 'Celestial Police' started a search for a missing planet. From the distances of the then-known planets, there seemed to be a suspiciously empty 'gap' between Mars and Jupiter. In 1801 Italian astronomer Giuseppe Piazzi discovered the 'dwarf planet' Ceres in the gap – but almost by accident, as he was not a member of the 'police'. However over the following few years the 'police' found three asteroids – Pallas, Vesta and Juno.

Artists' views of the Main Belt often show the asteroids (smaller lumps) as close together, whereas really they are huge distances apart.

The great mass at the centre of the nebula came together to form the Sun. Smaller clumps formed the planets, including rocky ones like Earth and Mars, and gas giants such as Jupiter and Saturn. Even smaller rocky bits and pieces became the asteroids. They collected in the gap between Mars and Jupiter, probably pulled there by Jupiter's great gravity. So asteroids are 'leftovers' from the formation of the Solar System, too small to become proper planets. Sometimes they are called minor planets or planetoids.

The effect of being small

Because of their small size, most asteroids did not have enough gravity to form into ball-like shapes or spheres as they spun around. Many are shaped like lumpy potatoes. Unlike the planets of the Solar System, asteroids cannot hold a layer of gases or atmosphere around them.

Three belts

The Main Belt is made up of three belts, called the Inner, Middle and Outer Belts. There are gaps between these known as Kirkwood Gaps. Fewer asteroids orbit in the Kirkwood Gaps, due to the balance between the gravities of the Sun and Jupiter.

Space Facts

The Main Belt

● The Main Belt contains more than nine-tenths of all known asteroids.

● The Belt begins at about 300 million kilometres from the Sun. (The orbit of Mars averages 228 million kilometres from the Sun.)

● The Belt fades away by about 500 million kilometres from the Sun. (The orbit of Jupiter averages 779 million kilometres from the Sun.)

Asteroids Big and Small

The sizes of asteroids range from more than 500 kilometres across to tens of metres across. There are very few asteroids at the larger end of the scale, but as the sizes decrease, the number of asteroids increases. Scientists have discovered what asteroids are made of, as well as what they look like.

Asteroid size and mass

Around 220 asteroids are larger than 100 kilometres across. Pallas is the largest asteroid, measuring about 540 kilometres in length. The next largest is Vesta, which is only slightly smaller than Pallas. Vesta has a light-coloured surface and is the brightest asteroid when viewed from Earth.

The mass of an object is the amount of matter or substance in it. On Earth we measure it as weight. The total mass of all the known asteroids is less than three billion billion tonnes. This is tiny for space objects – only 1/25th of the mass of the Moon.

Many asteroids have bowl-like craters where they have bumped into one another.

SPACE DATA

The biggest asteroids are:

	Length or diameter
Pallas	540 kilometres
Vesta	530 kilometres
Hygiea	430 kilometres
Interamnia	340 kilometres
Davida	325 kilometres

What are asteroids made of?

Unlike the glowing gas tail of a comet (see page 7), asteroids do not give off their own light. Like the planets and moons, they shine by bouncing back or reflecting sunlight. Studies of the light reflected by asteroids, as well as the evidence collected by flypasts and visits by spacecraft, have revealed that asteroids are mostly rock and/or metal. Some asteroids are rich in carbonaceous (carbon-based) rock. Some contain more silicaceous (silicon-based) rock such as quartz – familiar on Earth as sand grains. The M-type asteroids are mainly metals, especially iron or iron-nickel.

Gaspra was the first asteroid to be visited by a space probe, Galileo, in 1991.

Most asteroids have surfaces pockmarked with gouges, scars and circular bowl-like shapes called craters. These marks have been made by past collisions, mostly with other asteroids and meteoroids. Since an asteroid has no atmosphere, there is no weathering or wearing down of the surface as there is on Earth, so the marks stay for huge spans of time. The surface appearance will only change as a result of further collisions.

Space Facts

Discovering asteroids

● Many thousands of asteroids have been discovered and given names and numbers. For example the biggest asteroid, Pallas, is known as 2 Pallas, and Eros is known as 433 Eros.

● There could be two million asteroids which are one kilometre or larger.

● The total number of asteroids in the Main Belt is probably many millions.

Asteroids Near and Far

Asteroids take several years to orbit the Sun – longer than their neighbouring planet nearer the Sun, Mars, but shorter than the next planet out, Jupiter. Asteroids also spin around, like the planets. Apart from the Main Belt asteroids, there are asteroids elsewhere in the Solar System. Many of these are near to other planets, probably held there by each planet's pull of gravity balanced with the Sun's gravity.

A computer-coloured map of Vesta shows its highest mountains as white, then going lower through red, yellow, green and blue, to the deepest valleys as black.

Asteroid movements

Most asteroids in the Main Belt take between three and six years to orbit the Sun. For example, Vesta goes around once in about 3 years and 7 months. This time is one 'year' for Vesta, so it is more than three and a half times longer than our own Earth year. It means that Vesta is moving through space at about 20 kilometres per second.

Vesta also spins or rotates quite fast for an asteroid, once every 5 hours 20 minutes. This time is the 'day' for an asteroid, compared to Earth's day of 24 hours. If you were on Vesta, you would see the Sun rise, then set, then rise again, all within 5 hours 20 minutes.

Asteroid families

Certain groups of asteroids orbit close together in clumps. These are known as asteroid families or Hirayama families, named after the Japanese astronomer Kiyotsugu Hirayama who identified the first main families in 1918. Each family is probably the result of a collision in the past, when one large asteroid broke into pieces or fragments. This also explains the irregular, lumpy nature of many smaller asteroids.

Away from the Main Belt

Hundreds of asteroids orbit the Sun but are not in the Main Belt. The Eureka asteroid group circles the Sun along the orbit of Mars, mostly following behind the planet. The first of them, Eureka itself, was discovered in 1990. An asteroid that shares the same orbit as a planet is called a Trojan asteroid, so the asteroids in the Eureka group are known as the Mars Trojans. There are also Trojans in the orbit of Jupiter (see panel), as well as Neptune Trojans.

Space Facts

Orbiting asteroids

- Many hundreds of asteroids orbit the Sun along the same path as the planet Jupiter. They are called the Jupiter or Jovian Trojans.

- They are in two main groups, one in front of the planet and one behind it.

- Each group is 60 degrees, or one-sixth of a circle, away from Jupiter. These sites are places where the gravities of Jupiter and the Sun balance each other.

- Discoveries in 2006 show that some of the Jupiter Trojans may be captured comets rather than asteroids.

Asteroids like Antiope are binary, which means there are two rocky objects orbiting the Sun, and twirling around each other at the same time.

Asteroids near Earth

Numerous asteroids orbit the Sun close to our home world, Earth. We can study these asteroids in more detail and even visit them with spacecraft – but they also present the threat of collision with our planet.

Close to home

The general name for asteroids that go around the Sun in orbits close to Earth's orbit is Near Earth Asteroids (NEAs). One group is the Amors. The asteroids in this group circle the Sun just outside the orbit of our home planet. They do not actually cross our orbital path, although some cross the orbit of the next planet outwards, Mars.

One Amor asteroid is Eros, which was visited by the *NEAR-Shoemaker* spacecraft from 2000 to 2001 (see page 23).

It is possible that the two tiny moons of Mars, Phobos and Deimos, were asteroids that have been 'captured' by the gravity of Mars. It is also possible that some NEAs are burned-out or extinct comets.

These computer-coloured views show Eros from different angles, as it rolls and tumbles through space.

Earth-crossers

The Amors do not pose a collision threat to Earth. But some NEAs do. These are asteroids whose orbits do cross our own planet's orbit and they are known as Earth-crossers or Earth-Crossing Objects (ECOs). There are two main groups of ECOs, the Atens and Apollos.

Why ECOs cross Earth's orbit

How can these asteroids cross Earth's orbit if they are going around the Sun like our planet? The orbits of planets and asteroids around the Sun are not perfect circles, but oval-like 'squashed circles' called ellipses. The Atens are mostly just inside Earth's orbit, but at the farthest point in their ellipses they cross to the outside of it. The Apollos are the reverse. They are usually outside Earth's orbit, but at the narrowest part of the ellipse they cross to the inside.

How do we know?

The fat banana

The first spacecraft dedicated to studying an asteroid was *NEAR-Shoemaker*. It reached Eros in 2000 and went into orbit around it. The probe's information and pictures showed that Eros was shaped like a 'fat banana' about 33 kilometres long, with a deep gouge on one side and a large crater on the other.

The NEAR-Shoemaker *probe finally landed on asteroid Eros on 12 February 2001.*

Collision with Earth?

If some asteroids have orbits that cross the orbit of Earth, could one smash into our planet at some time? If so, what would be the result? That depends …

What are the chances?

There are many estimates for the chance of an asteroid crashing into Earth. All are very remote, usually many billions to one. But given the immense time spans involved, over billions of years, a collision has almost certainly occurred in the past, and another is likely in the future. In 1989 there was a 'near-miss' as asteroid Asclepius passed 700,000 kilometres away (in terms of the vast distances of space that is very near indeed). In 2004 the smaller 2004 FH, about 30 metres across, came within 43,000 kilometres – eight times closer than the Moon.

In the movie Deep Impact, *one part of a comet hits Earth and causes some damage. A smallish asteroid impact would have a similar effect, but a big asteroid would be truly devastating.*

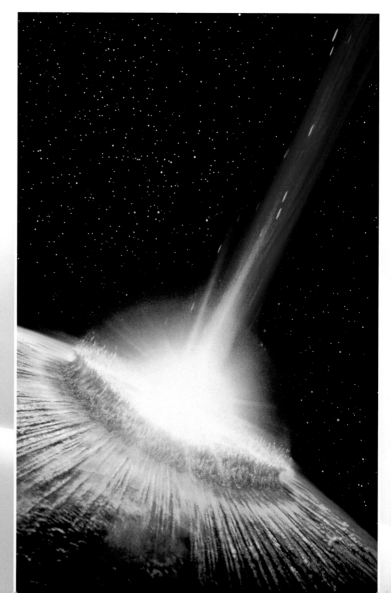

Space Fact

A possible collision

● In 2004 scientists worked out that asteroid 2004 MN4 (99942 Apophis) could crash into Earth in the year 2029. Further study showed that this was in fact unlikely. But a collision is still possible farther in the future, in 2036 or 2068.

An asteroid heading for Earth would start to heat up and glow as it entered the atmosphere (layer of air).

Impact disaster

If there is a collision, what happens depends on the size and speed of the asteroid, where it strikes Earth (land or sea, desert or mountains), and the angle of the impact. Any asteroid more than one kilometre across would probably cause global disaster. It would set off huge earthquakes and tsunamis (giant waves). It could throw dust or water droplets into the air that would blot out the Sun for months or years, leading to global cooling and plants withering in the gloom. Animals and people would then run out of food. It could be the end of human civilization as we know it.

Saving Earth

Many organizations keep watch for asteroids and other space objects approaching Earth (see page 39). If an asteroid appears to be on a collision course with Earth, what could we do? One possibility is to launch rockets equipped with nuclear explosives. These could blow up near the asteroid and knock it onto a different course, or even land on the asteroid and explode to crack it into pieces.

How do we know?

Asteroid damage on Earth

An asteroid collision may have wiped out the dinosaurs and many other animals and plants 65 million years ago. Rocks formed at this time on Earth contain unusually large amounts of the metal iridium. Iridium is rare on Earth, but common in asteroids. Scientists suggest that a 10-kilometre-wide asteroid smashed into what is now the sea off the Yucatan region of Mexico, blowing apart into billions of fragments which eventually settled on the ground and formed an iridium-rich layer of rock. A huge dip called the Chicxulub Crater under the sea-bed mud may be the site of the asteroid's impact.

Bodies Beyond Neptune

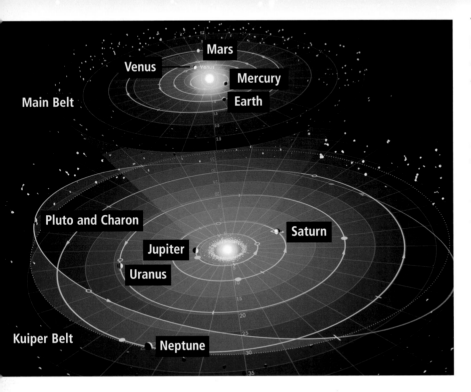

Venus
Mars
Mercury
Earth
Main Belt
Pluto and Charon
Saturn
Jupiter
Uranus
Kuiper Belt
Neptune

In the whole Solar System, the Sun and four inner planets are relatively close (central area, enlarged in gold). The four outer planets (blue) are much farther apart. The Kuiper Belt, with the dwarf planets Pluto and Charon (far left), is beyond Neptune (lower left).

The huge planet Neptune is the eighth planet of our Solar System – 30 times farther from the Sun than the Earth. Beyond Neptune is an area of the Solar System which is now being studied in more detail with the latest powerful telescopes and more advanced spacecraft.

The Kuiper Belt

Neptune is the outermost of the giant planets and its pull of gravity, interacting with the Sun's gravity, keeps various objects out there on the fringes of the Solar System, orbiting the Sun. The mysterious zone beyond Neptune is known as the Kuiper Belt. It is named after astronomer Gerard Kuiper, who first suggested its existence in 1950-51. The Belt probably finishes more than 7,000 million kilometres from the Sun, which is about 45-50 times the Earth-Sun distance.

Objects in the Kuiper Belt and beyond

There are thought to be huge numbers of objects in the Kuiper Belt, resembling asteroids, comets, planets and similar bodies. They have the general name of Kuiper Belt Objects (KBOs). Another name is Trans-Neptunian Objects (TNOs), which includes not only the objects in the Kuiper Belt but any that may be beyond it. Astronomers think there may be an even bigger doughnut-shaped zone of objects next to the Kuiper Belt, known as the Scattered Disc, which is probably outside what we regard as the Solar System.

Groups of KBOs

The first object classed as a KBO was asteroid-like and discovered in 1992. Its official name is 15760 1992 QB1 but it is usually just called 'QB1' or 'cubewan'. It has given its name to one group of KBOs, the cubewanos. Other types include the plutinos ('little Plutos'), which have features similar to Pluto, the former ninth planet of the Solar System.

No longer a planet

Pluto was discovered in 1930, and its relatively large moon, Charon, found in 1978. In 2006 the International Astronomical Union decided that there should be eight planets, stopping at Neptune. Both Pluto and Charon were put into a new group called the 'dwarf planets'. (The largest asteroid, Ceres, was also included as a 'dwarf planet'.)

An object larger than Pluto was discovered in the Kuiper Belt in 2003. Known as 2003 UB313, it has been named Eris. Hailed as the 'tenth planet' on its discovery, in 2006 it too was grouped with Pluto, Charon and Ceres, as a 'dwarf planet'. Doubtless in the years to come, many similar KBOs will join the 'dwarf planet' list.

The deep-space probe New Horizons, *launched 2006, is due to visit Pluto, Charon and other KBOs from 2015.*

Space Facts

The Kuiper Belt

● The inner edge of the Kuiper Belt is near the orbit of Neptune, almost 4,500 million kilometres from the Sun. The outer edge may extend more than 7,000 million kilometres from the Sun.

● The 'dwarf planet' Pluto's orbit is so 'squashed' into an ellipse that at its nearest to the Sun it is 4,435 million kilometres, and at its farthest, 7,300 million kilometres. This means Pluto crosses from the inside to the outside of the Kuiper Belt twice on each orbit.

The Three 'M's

Three terms beginning with 'm' are often confused. These are meteoroid, meteor and meteorite. One is found in space, the second in Earth's atmosphere and the third here on the ground.

Meteors are best seen at night, but sometimes show up at dawn or dusk.

Meteoroid

A meteoroid is a little lump or piece of rock in space, usually much smaller than an asteroid – ranging in size from a few metres across down to the size of a grain of sand or tinier. Meteoroids may have wandering, random or haphazard paths through space, rather than going around the Sun in regular orbits. Most meteorites are fragments of asteroids, comets, moons and other bodies which have been broken apart by collisions.

Meteor

A meteor is the streak of light which is formed as a meteoroid 'burns up' while entering Earth's atmosphere. It is often called a 'falling star' or 'shooting star'. Meteors occur high in the atmosphere, usually above 50 kilometres, which is far above the weather and clouds, and much higher than the typical cruising height of jet aircraft at around 10 to 12 kilometres.

How do we know?

Meteorite strikes

Through telescopes we can see impact craters caused by meteorite strikes on other planets, moons and asteroids. In 2005 the wheeled robot-like rover *Opportunity* on Mars found a piece of rock there about the size of a basketball. This has been named the Meridiani Planum meteorite (see opposite).

Meteorite

Most meteoroids burn up completely as meteors. But some are very large, or resistant to melting, or strike the atmosphere at a certain angle. They are not totally burned away. One or more pieces survive and fall onto the Earth's surface. These are meteorites. In fact, meteorites fall not only onto Earth, but onto other space objects too, including other planets, moons and asteroids. For example, many bowl-shaped pits called craters can be clearly seen on Mars and on Earth's Moon. These craters were made by meteorite impacts.

The Mars meteorite photographed by the Opportunity rover in January 2005, and nicknamed 'SpongeBob', is an iron-nickel meteorite.

Space Facts

Danger!

● Meteoroids are a constant danger to spacecraft, including satellites and long-distance space probes.

● When astronauts go on 'space walks' they wear spacesuits that are specifically designed to resist micrometeoroids. These are very small particles, smaller than a pinhead, which might otherwise puncture the suit and let the air leak out.

● One spacecraft in orbit for four years was struck by at least 79 micrometeoroids. The largest measured about 50 micrometres across, or 1/20th of one millimetre – about the width of a human hair.

Shooting Stars

Space Facts

Displays from debris

- Some meteors are caused not by natural objects from space, but by artificial items made by people. These objects include parts of old rockets, spacecraft and satellites which have been in Earth orbit but gradually arc down into the atmosphere.

- A spectacular display of meteors occurred when parts of the old Mir space station fell back to Earth in March 2001.

A sudden streak of light in the clear night sky is often called a 'shooting star' or 'falling star'. It is not a star at all, but a tiny piece of rock, a meteoroid, ending its immense journey through space as it burns up in the Earth's atmosphere.

Heat and light

The 'shooting star' trail or streak of light is a meteor. As a meteoroid zooms into the thickening layer of air around Earth, it rubs against the air particles (atoms and molecules). It also squashes the air particles in front of it by a process known as ram pressure. The rubbing or friction of air resistance and the ram pressure generate so much heat that the air begins to glow, while the meteoroid itself melts and turns to vapour. The light generated shows as a fast-moving streak across the dark sky.

Meteors at great heights can be photographed through telescopes.

As a rocky meteoroid approaches Earth and burns up in the thickening atmosphere, it leaves a trail of light called a meteor.

Millions every day

Millions of tiny meteoroids fall towards Earth every 24 hours as the planet races through space. They arrive at speeds of up to 70 kilometres per second. Those that come in daylight cannot be seen forming meteors, as the Sun is too bright. On clear nights the smallest burn up so high in the atmosphere, up to 100 kilometres high, that their glow is not visible from the ground. Slightly larger ones, about the size of the dot on this 'i', make it farther down into the atmosphere, but they have usually burned away by 50 kilometres high.

The fate of larger meteoroids depends on how fast they travel, the angle at which they meet Earth's atmosphere, and their chemical make-up (see page 35). Some cause much brighter glows or trails and may heat up so quickly that they burn fast as 'fireballs', or even explode in a bright flash, known as a bolide.

Space Fact

Light trails

● The length of a meteoroid's light trail and how long it lasts depend on the meteoroid's size and chemical make-up. Small, fast-moving particles form light trails that last just a few seconds, while larger meteoroids can produce a glow lasting for more than half an hour.

Meteor Showers and Storms

On average, a meteor happens every few seconds somewhere around the Earth. But at certain times they become much more common, and the clear night sky seems alive with streaks and flashes. These are meteor showers, or if there are even more light trails, meteor storms.

Long ago people often linked meteor showers – along with eclipses and comets – to the anger of gods or the wrath of spirits. By the 1900s scientists had worked out why meteors sometimes come in showers or storms. The usual reason is that the Earth, on its long orbit around the Sun, is passing through tiny bits of dust and debris left by a long-gone comet. These remnants 'hang' like a dusty streamer in space, tracing the comet's orbit. Each time the Earth comes around, it encounters some of the particles.

Yearly showers

Because the Earth orbits the Sun once each year, these meteor showers occur at predictable times of the year. For example, the Perseid shower is usually around 11-12 August (see panel on page 33). It is caused by dust and debris from a comet that passed in 1862. The Eta Aquarids of May and the Orionids of October happen when Earth passes through the debris, or orbital dust cloud, left by Halley's Comet.

This photograph of the Leonid shower, taken over many minutes, shows ordinary stars moving as slightly curved streaks. The meteors seem to burst out from one area called the radiant (middle right).

Parallel movement

Imagine looking along a multi-lane highway into the distance. The vehicles are moving parallel to each other. But to the viewer, they seem to come from one distant spot and get farther apart as they come nearer. In the same way, the streaks of light in a meteor shower seem to 'explode' from one place in the sky. In fact they are also moving parallel to each other. The spot where they seem to originate is known as the radiant. The constellation (pattern of stars) where the radiant lies gives its name to the meteor shower. The Perseid shower originates from Perseus. The Leonid shower, due to the comet Tempel-Tuttle (see page 10), originates from Leo. (Perseus is nearly overhead at about 10 pm in Europe/North America in January, and Leo is down near the horizon looking east at the same time and place.)

The Moon has no atmosphere, so when a meteoroid crashes there, it does not slow down or leave a trail of light.

Night spectacle

Meteor showers and storms make a spectacular sight, and people gather at popular viewing points away from city lights to admire the display. In a typical shower there are between 5 and 60 meteors every hour – that is, up to one each minute. But some heavy showers or storms peak at one meteor every second. These meteor 'downpours' can affect radio, television and long-distance communications by producing bursts of energy high in the atmosphere.

SPACE DATA

Some main meteor showers:

Name of shower	Date of peak
Quadrantids	3 January
Eta Aquarids	4 May
Delta Aquarids	29 July
Perseids	11-12 August
Orionids	20-21 October
Leonids	16-17 November
Geminids	13 December

Crashing into Earth

Only a tiny fraction of meteoroids survive their journey through the Earth's atmosphere and reach the surface as meteorites. Rarely a large meteorite smashes into the ground and causes great damage. But most meteorite impacts are small and go unnoticed.

Falling speed

As meteorites fall through the thickening atmosphere, increasing air resistance makes them move slower and slower. Most smaller ones do not smash into the ground like speeding bullets fired from a powerful gun. Instead they slow down when they reach Earth's atmosphere and end up simply 'falling', at a speed where the pull of Earth's gravity bringing them down is balanced by the air's resistance to their movement. Their impact speed is about 100-150 metres per second – around four times faster than a car on the highway.

A piece of one of the largest meteorites ever found on Earth is displayed at the American Museum of Natural History in New York City, USA.

Larger meteorites, usually those containing plenty of iron, may have enough mass to keep some of the speed they had in space, and so they hit the ground harder. This applies even more to asteroids, which are even bigger. The impact speed of even a small asteroid could be up to 10,000 metres per second, and a larger one twice as fast.

The effect of a meteorite impact (see page 36) depends not only on its size and speed, but also on the angle it strikes the ground, and the nature of the ground. Soft soil or mud soaks up the energy of the impact, so there are few lasting effects.

A magnified view of a meteorite shows tiny colourful lumps of minerals, mostly up to one millimetre across.

Types of meteorites

For many years meteorites have been put in one of three groups:

- Stony (rocky) with silicate minerals.

- Iron (metallic), usually mixed iron and nickel, with about nine-tenths iron.

- Mixed, with both stony minerals and iron-based metals.

Newer ways of grouping them depend on their more detailed chemical make-up and whether or not they contain tiny ball-shaped lumps of minerals known as chondrules. Those which have chondrules are known as chondrites, and those without are achondrites. Studying the make-up of meteorites helps scientists to understand the objects from which they came, such as asteroids or comets.

Great Meteorite Strikes

Once every million years or so, Earth is probably hit by a small asteroid or large meteorite which has global effects. Smaller meteorite impacts are more common, perhaps leaving a crater several hundred metres across. But over time the Earth's wind, rain and weather wear away the rocks. Plants grow and soil, sand or mud collect. So gradually the signs of these impact craters disappear.

Classic crater

One of the most striking and well-shaped impact craters is the Barringer or Meteor Crater (Canyon Diablo Crater) near Winslow in Arizona, USA. It is about 1,260 metres across, 180 metres deep and surrounded by a rim 45 metres high. It was probably formed about 50,000 years ago by a meteorite almost 50 metres across, weighing up to 300,000 tonnes, which exploded when it hit the ground. The crater left by the impact has been preserved so well because of the dry desert conditions.

A mysterious explosion

In 1908 a huge explosion shook the region of Tunguska, in Siberia. No crater was formed. But the damage was immense, with trees blasted over and other shock-wave damage over an area of 4,000 square kilometres. One explanation is that a meteorite (or perhaps a piece of comet) about 30 metres across exploded at a height of 10 kilometres as it hurtled down at an angle of about 45 degrees.

One of the biggest, best-preserved meteorite craters is the Barringer Crater in Arizona, USA.

Space Facts

A meteorite from Mars

- In 1996 scientists studying a meteorite from Antarctica decided that it had come from Mars. It was perhaps knocked off the planet's surface by another meteorite strike.

- Known as ALH84001, the Martian meteorite apparently had microscopic worm-like 'fossils' in it. This suggested that Mars supported some form of life long ago.

- However other scientists claim that the 'fossils' are simply natural formations of minerals in the rock.

The 'fossils' in Mars meteorite ALH84001 could be remains of microscopic life-forms, like bacteria on Earth.

Famous meteorites

The biggest known meteorite on Earth is the Hoba meteorite of Namibia (see panel). The Willamette meteorite first studied by scientists in Oregon, USA in 1902 is about 3 metres long and weighs 14 tonnes. The Cape York meteorite from Greenland's west coast, discovered in 1897, weighs almost 31 tonnes and was taken to New York City for display.

SPACE DATA

The Hoba meteorite

Found: 1920, near Grootfontein, Namibia, south-west Africa.

Size: about 2.7 metres by 2.3 metres.

Weight: estimated at almost 60 tonnes.

How We Observe Comets, Asteroids and Meteors

Compared to looking at planets such as Jupiter and Saturn, searching for small space bodies like comets and asteroids is difficult and chance-ridden. But new telescopes and spacecraft, as well as more powerful computers, are discovering more small space objects at an ever-increasing rate.

Keeping watch

The lone amateur studying the night sky still has a chance of finding a comet or asteroid, or noticing a new meteor shower. But today's professional astronomers belong to big organizations involved in the lookout for new asteroids, comets and similar objects. In particular, 'asteroid-watching' has become an exciting business, since one day an asteroid could be spotted which is on a collision course with Earth. The people who find it will then become the focus for world attention and saving our planet as they will have alerted everyone to the approaching danger.

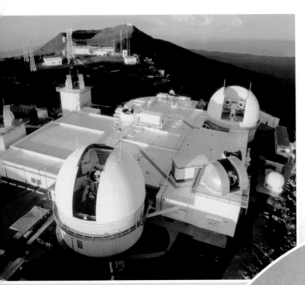

The telescope-housing domes and buildings nicknamed 'Science City' on Maui, Hawaii, are part of the NEAT asteroid-watching system.

How do we know?

Testing radioactivity

Rocks and fossils on Earth are tested in various ways to show when they formed. These tests include detecting the amount of radiation energy – radioactivity – the rocks contain. Meteorites can be tested in the same way to find their age. Comets and asteroids can also be tested, by spacecraft that land on them or collect their dust and fragments from space. Some meteorites, comets and bits of asteroids have been dated at billions of years old. They give clues to the nature of rocky objects in space soon after the Solar System formed. One of the oldest is the Krahenberg meteorite, which could go back more than 4,500 million years almost to the 'birth' of the Solar System.

The Kitt Peak National Observatory in Arizona, USA, has more than 20 telescopes which have discovered many hundreds of comets and asteroids.

For their space surveys, professional astronomers use massively powerful telescopes which automatically scan the sky, taking thousands of pictures every night. Most are wide-field optical telescopes which see a large part of the sky, rather than a tiny part highly magnified.

Computer-powered searches

Pictures are taken through the telescopes by digital cameras, and fed into supercomputers. These automatically compare the pictures with each other and with pictures in the memory banks, to find objects that are new or moving in an unusual way. Using this method, thousands of asteroids are discovered every month. The results are coordinated by several organizations such as NASA, the US National Aeronautics and Space Administration, and Spaceguard (see panel). They share out sky-scanning so as much of space as possible is viewed each night.

Space Facts

Asteroid-watchers

● LINEAR, the Lincoln Near-Earth Asteroid Research programme, has its base near Socorro, New Mexico, USA.

● LONEOS, the Lowell Observatory Near-Earth Object Search, is also looking out for Earth-Crossing asteroids and comets. It is based at the Lowell Observatory near Flagstaff, Arizona, USA.

● NEAT, the Near-Earth Asteroid Tracking set-up, is organized by NASA's JPL (Jet Propulsion Laboratory) from Pasadena, California, USA. It has two main telescope locations at the Maui Space Surveillance Site on the island of Maui, Hawaii, and the Palomar Observatory in California, USA.

● Spacewatch is based at the University of Arizona's Lunar and Planetary Laboratory in Tucson, Arizona, USA.

● CINEOS, the Campo Imperatore Near Earth Object Survey, has its headquarters at the Rome Observatory, Italy.

● Spaceguard is an international group working with bodies such as the European Space Agency, the United Nations and the organizations listed here. It has telescopes in many countries, including Japan, Australia and the UK.

How We Explore Comets, Asteroids and Meteors

Many space probes have headed out into deep space to fly past or land on comets, asteroids and other small space objects. Some take 'normal' photographs using light. Others use radio waves to detect size and shape, or pick up rays and waves from the object, such as infra-red (heat) rays and even X-rays. All of this information is changed into radio waves to send back to Earth.

Meeting comets

The first deep-space craft to fly past a comet was *ICE*, the *International Cometary Explorer*. After launch in 1978 it went near to Comet Giacobini-Zinner in 1985, on its way to Halley's Comet in 1986. Halley's Comet was also viewed by several other craft including *Giotto* (see page 9). Other comet-visiting craft are *Stardust*, which

flew past asteroid Annefrank and close to Comet Wild 2; *Deep Space 1* (launched in 1998), *Rosetta* (2004) and *Deep Impact* (2005).

Another probe, *CONTOUR* (*Comet Nucleus Tour*) was launched in 2002 with the aim of visiting the Comets Encke in 2003, Schwassmann-Wachmann 3 in 2006 and d'Arrest in 2008. Sadly contact with it was lost when boosting out of Earth orbit.

Deep Impact's 'lander' or impactor smashed into Comet Tempel 1 at an incredible speed of 10,000 metres per second.

Asteroid visits

In 1991 the far-travelling *Galileo* probe travelled past the asteroids Gaspra and Ida, on its way to the giant planet Jupiter. It discovered the first moon orbiting an asteroid when it detected Dactyl going around Ida.

NASA's car-sized *NEAR-Shoemaker* (*Near Earth Asteroid Rendezvous*, see pages 22-23) set off in 1996. It passed by the Main Belt asteroid Mathilde the following year, taking pictures that showed it was one of the blackest objects ever seen in space.

In November 2005 the Hayabusa *craft landed briefly on the small asteroid Itokawa, which is only about 540 metres long.*

After several problems, *NEAR-Shoemaker* made a 'swingby' pass back near Earth, so that it could use Earth's gravity to redirect its course, approaching to just 540 kilometres. It then headed off again to orbit around the Near Earth asteroid Eros in 2000. It landed on the surface of Eros in 2001 and sent back 69 close-up pictures. Finally, two weeks after landing the probe was shut down. Like other landers on similar space objects, it is still there.

41

The Future

Over the coming years, telescopes will continue to scan the skies for exciting new comets, spectacular meteor showers and the worrying threat of a suddenly-detected asteroid heading for our world. Also several space probes are on their way, or planned for launch, to visit small objects in deep space.

In 2005 Rosetta came within 1,500 kilometres of Earth on a 'flypast', before heading out to encounter asteroids and comets.

Current and future missions

The European Space Agency's *Rosetta* space probe was launched in 2004. The first part of its mission is to study the Main Belt asteroids Steins in 2008 and Lutetia in 2010. Then after 'hibernating' to save energy for three years it is due to meet up with Comet Churyumov-Gerasimenko in 2014. A lander called *Philae* will touch down softly on the comet's surface, as the main probe orbits and then follows the comet's path. Together they will monitor the deep-frozen comet as it heads towards the Sun, warms up, 'switches on', and loops around the Sun in 2015.

The NASA space agency's *Dawn* mission in 2007 is to the Main Belt. It should orbit the large asteroid Vesta in 2011 and then the 'dwarf planet' Ceres (formerly regarded as the biggest asteroid) in 2015.

Looking out

The coming years will see continued space surveys and asteroid-watching for any object likely to threaten planet Earth. There will also be new comets, unpredictably appearing as if from nowhere. Long into the future it may be possible to send craft to asteroids and meteorites, to mine their metals and minerals which are very rare on Earth and return these valuable resources to our home planet.

New Horizons

One of the most ambitious and the most complex of all space probes is *New Horizons*. It left Earth in 2006 on an immense journey to Pluto and then the Kuiper Belt. In the meantime telescopes here on Earth will continue to improve and be able to peer out to the distant edge of the Solar System in more detail. Some astronomers expect to discover swarms of exciting new objects in the Kuiper Belt, the Scattered Disc and beyond. The former view that the Solar System 'ended' at the planet Pluto has already changed greatly. Pluto is no longer regarded as a true planet. We also know there are vast numbers of objects beyond it, including comets and various asteroid-like objects – whose numbers may be in the millions, or even billions.

Far in the future, 'asteroid mining' to obtain rare and valuable minerals may become possible. But saving Earth's own resources would be far cheaper and less dangerous.

The *New Horizons* mission plan:

2006	Launch from Earth
	Fly past Main Belt asteroid JF56
2007	Fly past Jupiter for gravity-assist boost
2015	Visit Pluto and Charon
	Closest approach to Pluto, 10,000 kilometres
2016	Continue through Kuiper Belt, locating and studying KBOs
2025	Shutdown

Timeline of Discovery

65 million years ago A massive meteorite or asteroid may have struck Earth, causing a global catastrophe that wiped out the dinosaurs and many other animals and plants.

50,000 years ago The Barringer or Meteor Crater (Canyon Diablo Crater) in Arizona, USA was formed by an impact; it was discovered by scientists in 1871.

1070s Halley's Comet was pictured on the Bayeux Tapestry depicting the Battle of Hastings and the Norman invasion of England in 1066.

1492 The first scientific record of a meteorite fall in modern times was made in Ensisheim, Alsace.

1801 Giuseppe Piazzi observed Ceres, which was first believed to be a planet, then became the first asteroid to be officially discovered, and then in 2006 was 'promoted' again to become a dwarf planet.

1802 The second asteroid was discovered, Pallas. Juno followed in 1804 and Vesta in 1807.

Devastation in the aftermath of the explosion in Tunguska, Siberia, in 1908.

1845 Postmaster and amateur astronomer Karl Hencke discovered Astraea, the fifth asteroid to be found, almost 40 years after the fourth.

1906 Max Wolf discovered the first of the Trojan asteroids following the same path as planet Jupiter.

1908 A huge explosion in Tunguska, Siberia, caused immense damage; it may have been a meteoroid or piece of comet that exploded several kilometres above the ground.

1932 The first Earth-crossing asteroid, Apollo, was discovered.

1947   The second-biggest "meteoroidal event" of the 20th century (after Tunguska) occurred in Sikhote-Alin, eastern Russia. A meteorite exploded at a height of about five kilometres and the largest fragments made small pits and craters.

1950   Astronomer Fred Whipple suggested his 'dirty snowball' theory for the make-up of a comet.

1950   Jan Oort suggested that comets might come from a gigantic 'shell' of objects far beyond the Solar System, now known as the Oort Cloud.

1951   Gerard Kuiper suggested the existence of swarms of objects beyond planet Neptune, in the zone now called the Kuiper Belt.

1986   Halley's Comet came near to Earth; its next visit is in 2061.

1994   Parts of Comet Shoemaker-Levy 9 plunged into the giant planet Jupiter.

The New Horizons *probe.*

1998   The *Deep Space 1* craft was launched and travelled past three comets in three years.

2001   *NEAR-Shoemaker* spacecraft visited the near-Earth asteroid Eros and showed it looked like a 'fat banana'.

2004   The *Stardust* space probe passed by Comet Wild 2 and collected samples of its coma.

2004   The *Rosetta* space probe set off to meet asteroids in the Main Belt in 2008 and 2010, then Comet Churyumov-Gerasimenko in 2014.

2005   A small 'impactor' from spacecraft *Deep Impact* smashed into the surface of the nucleus of Comet Tempel 1.

2006   The *New Horizons* probe set off to the edge of the Solar System, on a 20-year mission to visit Pluto and other objects in the Kuiper Belt.

Glossary

asteroid A rocky object that orbits the Sun, but that is not large enough to be a planet.

astronomer A scientist who specializes in the study of space.

chondrules Tiny ball-like, glassy lumps of minerals, usually rich in silica, found in certain kinds of meteorites.

coma In a comet, the glow that surrounds the core or nucleus of the head region.

comet A small, icy object that comes near to the Sun.

crater A dish-shaped hole in the surface of a planet, moon or other space object.

ECO Earth-Crossing Object, a space object such as an asteroid that cross the path of Earth's orbit.

gravity A pulling or attracting force possessed by all objects, mass and matter.

Kuiper Belt A ring-like area of the Solar System beyond the planet Neptune, but not as far out as the Oort Cloud.

Main Belt Another name for the Asteroid Belt between Mars and Jupiter, where most asteroids are found.

mass Matter or substance, in terms of the numbers and types of atoms or other tiny particles.

meteor A streak or flash of light, often called a 'shooting star' or 'falling star', caused by a meteoroid burning up as it enters Earth's atmosphere.

meteor shower Many meteors that occur close together.

meteorite A small, usually rocky particle from space that crashes onto the surface of a planet, moon or other space body.

meteoroid A piece of rock, metal or similar substance, smaller than an asteroid, that moves through space.

NEA Near Earth Asteroid, an asteroid that orbits relatively close to our planet.

nonperiodic comet A comet that passes the Sun once and heads away into deep space.

nucleus In a comet, the small, rocky centre or core inside the 'head'.

observatory (astronomical observatory) A building or place, usually with telescopes and similar equipment, where people study objects in space.

Oort Cloud An immense ball-like 'shell' of space objects, including perhaps billions of comets, that surrounds the Solar System at a vast distance.

orbit The path of one object going around another, such as a planet around the Sun, or a moon around a planet.

periodic comet A comet that goes around or orbits the Sun on a regular journey.

probe A spacecraft launched into space to send back information about objects such as asteroids and comets.

radiant The place in the sky from which the meteors in a meteor shower all seem to come from.

radiation Energy that spreads out or radiates from its source, often in the form of rays or waves.

Scattered Disc A doughnut-shaped region of space beyond the Kuiper Belt, where many objects may occur.

tail In a comet, a long stream of gas or dust that points away from the Sun (rather than trailing along behind the comet).

Trojan asteroid An asteroid that follows the same path or orbit as a planet.

Further Information

Books

Asteroids, Comets and Meteors (Worlds Beyond) Ron Miller, 21st Century, 2004

National Geographic Encyclopedia of Space Linda K. Glover
National Geographic Society, 2005

Organizations

National Aeronautics & Space Administration (NASA)
Organization that runs the US space program
www.nasa.gov

International Astronomical Union (IAU)
The official world astronomy organization, responsible for naming stars, planets, moons and other objects in space
www.iau.org

International Meteor Organization
Produces calendars and advice on meteors, showers and storms, and the scientific journal WGN
www.imo.net/

Spaceguard
Dedicated to keeping watch for asteroids, comets and other space objects that could be a threat to Earth
spaceguard.esa.int/

Jet Propulsion Laboratory (JPL)
Centre responsible for NASA's robot space probes
www.jpl.nasa.gov

European Space Agency (ESA)
Organization responsible for space flight and exploration by European countries
www.esa.int

The Planetary Society
Organization devoted to the exploration of the Solar System
www.planetary.org

Websites

www.spds.nasa.gov/planetary/planets/asteroidpage.html
NASA's information and fact sheets on asteroids.

spaceplace.nasa.gov/en/kids/deepimpact/deepimpact.shtml
The story of Deep Impact's visit to comet Tempel 1.

http://www.ast.cam.ac.uk/~jds/
The comets section of the British Astronomical Society and Society for Popular Astronomy, with the latest news and sightings.

cfa-www.harvard.edu/icq/icq.html
International Comet Quarterly has news, observations, orbital data, designations and names, and links regarding comets and related topics, run by the Harvard-Smithsonian Center for Astrophysics.

www.meteorobs.org/index.html
Lists, advice and news on how to watch meteors from MeteorObs.

Index

Numbers in **bold** indicate pictures.

THE EARTH AND SPACE

Contents of titles in the series: